Beale H. Richardson

Pleasure Guide for Northern Tourists and Invalids

Beale H. Richardson

Pleasure Guide for Northern Tourists and Invalids

ISBN/EAN: 9783337193713

Printed in Europe, USA, Canada, Australia, Japan

Cover: Foto ©Andreas Hilbeck / pixelio.de

More available books at **www.hansebooks.com**

FOR

NORTHERN TOURISTS AND INVALIDS.

SKETCH OF THE RESORTS

ON

SAVANNAH, SKIDAWAY & SEABOARD RAILROAD

AND ITS BRANCHES,

BY

B. H. RICHARDSON,

CITY EDITOR MORNING NEWS.

SAVANNAH, GA:
MORNING NEWS STEAM JOB PRINT.
1875.

THE CITY OF SAVANNAH

AND HER

SUBURBAN RESORTS AND POINTS OF LOCAL INTEREST.

HOW TOURISTS MAY SPEND A PLEASANT SEASON.

Savannah's Advantages as a Winter Resort for Invalids.

The annual increase of travel to the South of pleasure seekers and invalids, and the eager search for information in regard to points of interest and accommodations, render it necessary that some light should be thrown upon the subject, especially so far as Savannah is concerned, in order that strangers may be advised of the attractions possessed by the Forest City. During several years past it is estimated that between fourteen and fifteen thousand persons have stopped in Savannah *en route* to the Flowery Land, which seems to be the *ultima Thule* of their fondest dreams of recreation, repose and amusement. It can scarcely be doubted that if these annual visitors were correctly informed of the advantages of our city as a winter resort, they would be induced to prolong their stay, possibly to abandon altogether their journey further.

With this belief, the management of the Savannah, Skidaway and Seaboard Railroad Company present the following little sketch of the various pleasure resorts along the main line and branches of their road, which resorts have been pronounced by strangers who have visited them, as possessing natural beauty that can scarcely be equalled in grandeur and magnificence. An additional attraction is given these points by their historical interest. That this sketch may be complete, it is necessary to commence with a brief notice of

SAVANNAH,

the commercial emporium of the Empire State of the South, beautifully situated on the Savannah River, about eighteen miles from its mouth. The picturesque appearance of the city impresses every visitor. It is hansomely laid out, with broad streets, closely shaded by water oaks, live oaks, magnolia, sycamore and pride of India trees. South Broad and Liberty streets have grassy promenades in the middle, with carriage ways on either side. The city has many fine buildings, several possessing considerable architectural merits, and a park which is the pride of the citizens and the admiration of strangers. The hotel accommodations are ample, and the General Ticket Agent of the Savannah, Skidaway and Seaboard Railroad Company, Mr. R. R. Bren, 21 Bull Street, will furnish all who desire it, information as to where good board can be obtained at private residences, a register of such places being kept on file at his office.

As regards health and climate, no city in the south offers superior advantages to Savannah.

ISLE OF HOPE,

the terminus of the main line of the Savannah, Skidaway and Seaboard Railroad, is six and a half miles from Savannah, on the Skidaway River, and is famous for the magnificence of its natural scenery, and delightful situations. It was settled in 1732 (four years after the town of Savannah was founded), by three persons, Henry Parker, who took the northern third, John Fallowfield, who took the middle third, and Noble Jones, the southern third, the whole containing about fifteen hundred acres, and being equally divided among them. In the London Journal of 1744, an English tourist published an interesting account of his travels through Georgia, specially noting a visit to Noble Jones's place, at Isle of Hope (known as Wormsloe), and describing in vivid language the charming beauty of the place, the fine improvements and fortified residence of the owner, ruins of which yet can be seen by the visitor of to-day.

In 1763, Fallowfield's tract having reverted to the Crown, was granted to Noble Jones, and on that grant all the titles to the land at and near the present Railroad terminus now depend, It included the property of Dr. S. F. DuPont on the north, and extended to the Wormsloe line on the south, being known as Wimberly until very recently.

About the year 1809, it was divided among the heirs of Mrs. Sarah Glen, the grand-daughter of Noble Jones, and from them by purchase came into the possession of the present owners.

The Parker tract, beginning at Dr. DuPont's line, and forming the northern third, was divided among the heirs of the late Dr. James Parker, about the year 1842, and was first called Parkersville.

The Island is in the form of a horse shoe, and the visitor thus has from almost any point a sweeping view of the entire tract. Previous to the war, the only communication with Savannah was by means of a dirt road winding through a magnificent forest, which in the summer was redolent with the perfume of the fragrant jessamine. The road is yet used and is in good condition, though the completion of the Savannah, Skidaway and Seaboard Railroad, offering up a safe and rapid communication with the city, lessened the travel over it considerably.

From a straggling settlement the place has grown to the proportions of a respectable village, and is the summer home of some our best citizens, whilst many reside there the entire year round, the Isle being so well protected that the thermometer shows a more temperate range than in the city.

The waters in the immediate vicinity abound with oysters, crabs, hard shell and soft shell, shrimp, prawn and fish in season, and visitors can have these luxuries served up fresh from their native element, on short notice. A comfortable establishment, finely located, and just at the terminus of the road, offers ample accommodations to all. A bowling alley, billiard saloon and dancing hall are attached to the premises, and in close proximity is a saloon provided with the best wines and cigars to be obtained at any of the city establishments. Immediately in front of this hotel, a mammoth platform, covered and railed in, extending from the bluff over the water, 60 by 80 feet, has been constructed. Around this platform (the roof of which is composed of palmetto branches which flourish in the vicinity) are arranged comfortable seats. Beneath and at the extremity of the platform, three bath houses are erected, connected with dressing rooms in such a manner that the utmost privacy is secured. This is a new attraction added the present season, and which was required by the rapid increase in number of visitors to the resort. A short distance from this point, in a beautiful grove of mammoth oaks, draped in hanging veils of Spanish moss, is another platform for dancing. At and around these umbrageous oaks are placed circular seats or benches, whilst on the river bank immediately in front, conveniently arranged, are rustic seats, where one can sit in sweet serenity and contemplate the goodly scene.

> "The river like a silvery snake lays out
> His coil in the sunshine."

It breathes of freshness in the grove of noble oaks, wavy moss, and fragrant odors of jessamine and violet.

In an air line the Isle of Hope is only four miles from the ocean, and is directly opposite Skidaway Island, which, under the patronage of the Benedictine Fathers, will ere long become a blooming garden and a prosperous village. This Island is the site of the Catholic Industrial School, established for the benefit of the colored people belonging to the Church, and where not only their moral and educational culture receives attention, but habits of industry and frugality are taught them. The Island is easily accessible to visitors at Isle of Hope. In the vicinity are numerous other points of interest, including the ruins of the fortified residence at "Wormsloe," built during the Revolutionary war on a strictly military plan; at the northern extremity of the Isle there yet remains the battery erected during the late War between the States, and manned by the Confederate troops assigned for the protection of the coast.

The avenue through the forests bordering the Isle afford delightful promenades to those who find pleasure in communing with nature in her most attractive guise.

Not only as a place of visitation, but as a winter residence, Isle of Hope is one of the most charming and beautiful rural retreats to be found throughout the South, and the enterprise of the Savannah, Skidaway and Seaboard Railroad Company, to whom its present development is largely due, will be directed to. rendering it more attractive and desirable. A hotel is in contemplation, but in the meantime accommodations for a limited number can be obtained.

BETHESDA,

on the branch road running from Sandfly Station to Montgomery, is a beautiful tract of land, about eight miles from Savannah. The name signifies a "House of Mercy," and such it may in truth be termed, as it is the site of the Orphan Home and School under the patronage of the Union Society.

Rev. George Whitfield, in 1739, secured a grant from the trustees in England for "five hundred acres of any vacant land he might select." Under this authority this tract was selected, and on the 25th of March, 1740, Mr. Whitfield, with his own hands, laid the first brick of the house, which he called Bethesda, and the name by which the place will ever be known. Through the assistance of Selina, Countess of Huntingdon, Whitfield was enabled to complete the Home and see it in successful operation. In 1770 he died, and in his will was found a clause devising Bethesda to the Countess, and she did all that was in her power to carry out his wishes. Shortly after his death, however, the buildings were struck by lightning and consumed. They were rebuilt, but in 1782, the British troops, previous to their evacuation, destroyed everything of value. At the death of Lady Huntingdon in 1791, the school was discontinued, and the State Government claimed it and committed it to the management of a board of trustees. In 1801 the school was reorganized, and was under fine headway; but in 1805, one of the wings was destroyed by fire, and a hurricane swept off the out buildings. The trustees were unable to build, and by act of Legislature, were authorized to sell the property and distribute the proceeds among the benevolent institutions of Savannah. This was done on the 12th of March, 1809. The Union Society, the oldest charitable organization in the State, in 1854 purchased 125 acres of the ancient Bethesda, and erected suitable buildings there for home and school purposes, and in January, 1855, the boys under their charge were removed to their new abode. Since then many improvements have been made, and the Bethesda of to-day is a monument to the practical benevolence of Savannah. The anniversary of the Society is celebrated on the 23d of April; on these occasions, the best people of the city attend *en masse*. The event is made of peculiar interest to the boys of the school, by an unusually fine dinner tendered them specially by the managers. The character of the institution may be inferred when the records show that several of the worthiest and most successful business men in the city and State have been inmates of Bethesda.

In the early spring the place is a marvel of natural beauty. Its historical character renders it well worth a visit.

BEAULIEU,

another charming resort located along the Vernon River, within a short distance of the branch track of the Savannah, Skidaway and Seaboard Railroad, in full view of Montgomery (the terminus of the branch) and within walking distance, was settled on the 21st of March, 1739, by William Stevens, the author of the early history of Georgia. He gave it the present name on account of the fancied resemblance of the place to Beaulie, a manor of His Grace, the Duke of Montgomery. By some the name was spelled Biewly; how it was changed to Beaulieu is not ascertained. Upon Stevens's settlement of the place, the few residents were constantly annoyed by predatory attacks from the Indians and Spaniards, and were compelled to fortify their huts in order to retain possession. The place was, during the Revolutionary war, occupied by a small force of British troops. On Sunday, the 12th of September, 1779, Colonel Thomas Pinckney, with a command of 1200 men, sent from the fleet of Count D'Estaing, in long boats, landed at Beaulieu, the British troops to the number of thirty retiring upon their approach. It is stated, owing to the men under Pinckney being exposed in the boats, that had this little handful of "red coats" made any resistance, a landing could not have been effected without very serious loss, and possibly the patriot forces might not have been enabled to accomplish their object at all. Several skirmishes between the opposing forces subsequently took place at and around Beaulieu.

The place is delightfully located, and is now the site of a number of beautiful residences. It is about seven miles from the ocean, and is in every respect a most charming location. The surroundings of the place are picturesque, and elicit admiration of all visitors.

BURNSIDES,

is a famous fishing and crabbing "ground" in the vicinity of this place, and during the season rarely a day passes that scores of the disciples of Isaak Walton, do not leave the city, tempted by the reward which is sure to follow their angling for the finny tribe.

MONTGOMERY,

the terminus of this branch, is considered by many the most delightful of the suburban resorts in the vicinity of Savannah. It was regularly settled in 1801, and since that time has grown to be quite a village. It is distant about ten miles from Savannah, and is the headquarters of the Regatta Association of Georgia, during the summer. All the Yacht races under the auspices of the Regatta Association take place at this point; the circuit being from Montgomery to Ossabaw Sound, (which divides the waters of South Carolina and Georgia) seven miles and a half and return.

The ocean is in full view from the commanding bluff, and the sight presented on a fair day is really magnificent. About twenty yards from the railroad track, in a grove of stately oaks of extraordinary grandeur, is a platform for dancing, and during the regatta and excursion seasons, is always occupied by merry throngs. A number of very handsome residences are located at this point, and some of the private grounds are models of artistic and natural beauty. A row of elegant little cottages has been projected, and will be completed in time for occupation the coming season. These cottages will be located about three hundred yards from the bluff, on a slight elevation, and will command a beautiful view of the river and surounding country. It is the intention of the owner to fix these cottages up comfortably and neatly, and to rent them out. A fine hotel eligibly located at this point, is also in contemplation, and will doubtless be completed in ample time for use the approaching season.

The Regatta Association have at this point, a very comfortable Club House, and are talking of making additional improvements to their property. Along the bluff, are beautiful avenues, shaded on either side by rows of water oaks, and no more attractive place for a promenade or stroll can scarcely be imagined. The woods in the back ground abound in jessamines and other wild flowers, and what can be more delightful than to recline in the shades of these noble old oaks, standing sentinels as it were upon the banks of the beautiful flowing river, whilst,

"Gentle gales,
    Fanning their odoriferous wings
    Dispense native perfumes
    And whisper whence they stole
    Those balmy spoils."

Montgomery, indeed is a point that every stranger should visit; and save only on very cold days, is as charming in the early fall, almost as when nature has assumed her greenest garb, and the southland is fanned by balmy zephers.

LAUREL GROVE CEMETERY,

another point of interest to all strangers, has, by the enterprise of the management of the Savannah, Skidaway & Seaboard Railroad Company, been made the terminus of a branch track, connecting with the main street line at the junction of Whitaker and Anderson Streets. This branch was completed on Friday, the 16th April, 1875, and on the following day was thrown open to travel, on which occasion, a complimentary trip by the management was extended over the line to the citizens generally, and a special car, containing the Board of Directors of the Company, the Mayor and City Council and invited guests, made the trip in the afternoon over the entire line, from Bay Street terminus to the gates of the Cemetery. The construction of this new route, is a great public convenience, and adds but another to the many points of interest brought within easy access to visitors by the Savannah, Skidaway & Seaboard Railroad Company.

Laurel Grove Cemetery, although not as grandly magnificent as the famous Bonaventure Cemetery, four miles from the city, is well worth a visit; a little sketch of it will prove interesting.

On the 9th May, 1853, Hon. R. Wayne, Mayor of Savannah, in accordance with ordinance previously adopted by Council, issued his proclamation closing the old or brick Cemetery on South Broad Street, as a burial ground, on the first of July ensuing.

The Ordinance adopted the 3d of June, 1852, set apart as a public Cemetery, a tract of land on Springfield plantation belonging to the city, as a public Cemetery, and conferred upon it the title "Laurel Grove." The place was enclosed with a neat railing, connecting with a pillar of granite at each of the corners. The interior was laid out in avenues, walks and lots; the plan of the same being furnished by James O. Morse, Civil Engineer.

The establishment of this Cemetery was rendered necessary by the crowded state of the Old Cemetery, a small area of ten acres, which had been a place of sepulture for more than one hundred years. The rapid extension of the city limits, made that cemetery almost a central position, and on the score of health, it was deemed advisable to provide another place beyond the bounds of the city for the repose of the dead.

Thus was Laurel Grove Cemetery selected, and the Council showed much judgment in the matter. The Cemetery is situated on high ground, and bounded on the southwestern border by low ground covered with native forest, and is a picturesque and beautiful spot, eminently fitted for a resting place after "life's fitful fever."

ITS DEDICATION.

On the 10th of November 1852, the Cemetery was formally dedicated with imposing ceremonies. It was decided to signalize the event, by the delivery of a Poem and Address, in addition to the usual religious services. In compliance with public request, Hon. R. M. Charlton and Hon. Henry R. Jackson consented to perform this duty.

A platform was erected for the speakers, the clergy, and for the Mayor and Aldermen of the city, and seats were provided for the audience. The elements were auspicious, as, to use the language of one of the local papers: "The glory of a superb day, and the autumn leaves falling near by, added their own softening influence to the scene."

The services were opened by a prayer from the Rev. Dr. Willard Preston, of the Independent Presbyterian Church, Hon. R. M. Charlton recited an eloquent and appropriate original poem, which was followed by a chaste and beautiful address by Hon. Henry R. Jackson. The ceremonies were then closed by an impressive prayer from the Rev. Dr. Lovick Pierce, of the Methodist Episcopal Church.

Laurel Grove has now been a Cemetery for nearly twenty-three years. The first interment was made in October, 1852, and since that time to December 31, 1874, twenty-two years and two months, the number reached 20,069, of which 10,726 were of black or colored persons. In the plan of the Cemetery, fifteen acres were partitioned off exclusively for the colored people.

As statistics of this character are always interesting, we may note that of the 20,069 interments, 2,065 were of persons who had died out of the city, and were brought from abroad. The smallest number of interments was in 1853, being 531, the largest in 1865, being 1920, these were of soldiers who had been killed or who died from disease, wounds etc., contracted in the war.

A portion of the Cemetery to the left, upon entering, is occupied by the graves of Confederate soldiers, numbering nearly fifteen hundred, the majority of whom are unknown. The Memorial Association of Savannah, have, for years, tended this sacred spot with jealous care, and through their exertions, neat mounds have been made over every grave, and marked by plain white headboards. In one section of this spot, is erected a neat arch, bearing the inscription, "Men of Gettysburg;" where are gathered the remains of a noble little band that had found a gallant death on that historic field. The twenty-sixth of April is devoted to the annual decoration of the graves of these honored dead, and on this occasion, the Cemetery is thronged with high and low, rich and poor, the banker and the artisan, all engaged in the performance of the holy work.

> "Fair woman comes; and gentle hand
> Brings laurels, bay and immortelle;
> No cause more just, if she approves,
> Than that for which "our heroes fell."

Many of the private lots are adorned with handsome monuments, and tastefully and beautifully laid off. The avenues are all well shaded. Comfortable seats will be found throughout the grounds, and as, from some unexplained cause, the desire appears universal among strangers, to inspect the cemeteries of the cities they visit, they can rest assured, that a trip to Laurel Grove, over the street line of the Savannah, Skidaway and Seaboard Railroad Company, and a stroll through the beautiful grounds, will be well repaid in what they see to interest them.

THE ATTRACTIONS OF SAVANNAH.

As remarked in the commencement of this sketch, few southern cities posess as great attractions as Savannah, in the matter of climate, location, numerous points of local interest and beautiful suburban surroundings. As regards climate, Savannah may be claimed as one of, if not the healthiest cities in the entire country. Statistics which are regarded as infalible in argument, sustain this claim. Especially is Savannah a desirable resort in the winter, for those who are sufferers from pulmonary diseases. It is an accepted fact in the medical world, that an equable temperature is as important to the unfortunate consumptive as warmth, and in this particular from the middle of February to the first of December, Savannah recomends itself remarkably, for during that period of nearly ten months of the year, the ranges of temperature are from

1

70 to 92 degees, and this variation of 22 degrees, is at all times very easy and gradual. During the last few years, owing to the admirable system of drainage adopted by the city, and the construction of mammoth sewers, beneath the principal streets, Savannah has been freer from malarial afflictions than any southern seaport city. The winter months are delightful, and as a general thing, the really cold days of the entire season, do not number a score. In January and December, it is often sufficiently pleasant in the household with raised windows and open doors. By February the peach trees and jessamine have put forth their blossoms, and in brief the entire winter season may be said not to exceed six weeks.

The plateau or plain upon which Savannah is located, is almost a level, being forty-eight feet above the level of the sea at the Pulaski House; fifty feet at the intersection of Montgomery and Gwinnett streets; and forty-six feet at the Park. The Savannah river, soon after passing the city, in its course to the ocean, is divided into numerous channels, by small islands of marsh, the beautiful and delicate green of which, interspersed in the waters, affords, when viewed from the northeastern extremity of the bluff, on a pleasant afternoon, one of the most attractive scenes imaginable. The mortuary records, which are published weekly, during the summer season, conclusively establish the fact of the remarkable general health of the city, and this condition of affairs is even improved as the fall approaches. The climate is dry, and chille and fevers, even on the outskirts of the city, which in years gone by, were considered extremely unhealthy, are now complaints comparatively unknown.

The Statistical Atlas of the United States, for 1874, compiled by Francis L. Watley, and but recently issued, is worth careful examination, by any who are sceptical in regard to the general health of Savannah. This work, which evinces a remarkable amount of labor and research, will demonstrate the correctness of all assertions in respect to the public health of Savannah, contained in this sketch. During the past several seasons, many northern invalids, who left home with the intention of spending the winter in Florida, have been so charmed with Savannah's genial climate, and attractive appearance, that they remained here, and have had no cause to regret it, as their winter's sojourn proved highly beneficial to them. Several of these strangers have bought property in and around Savannah, with the view of having a permanent home here, during the winter season. This statement we make authoritively.

POINTS OF ATTRACTION.

Believing that with these facts before them, all of which can be substantiated, every intelligent northerner, into whose hands this pamphlet may come, will be convinced of the benefits to health which can be derived by avoiding the terrible, severe winters of the north, and seeking a home, *pro tempore*, in our beautiful Forest City, it is now proposed to notice breifly, some of the many attractions, in which interest, pleasure and instruction may be found.

As the most important of the local attractions, may be mentioned

FORSYTH PARK,

which is located in the southern portion of the city, and is accessible by either of the street lines of the Savannah, Skidaway and Seaboard Railroad Company, passing directly by the enclosure, and also within pleasant walking distance of any of the hotels or boarding houses. The original park which is enclosed with a neat iron railing, contains twenty acres, is handsomely laid out in graveled walks, and is composed mostly of the natural growth of the forest. It is a great resort throughout the year, and will ever be attractive to our citizens and visitors. The centre of the Park is adorned with a magnificent mammoth fountain, after the style of the fountains in the Place de la Concord in Paris. In the northeastern section of the plat will be found a neatly constructed aviary, covered with blooming vines and fragrant flowers, which is the "home" of several noble specimens of the feathered tribe, including two large eagles, an owl, a large water crane, and several other birds.

A large plat of land immediately adjoining the Park, is enclosed, and is known as the Park extension, and in a few years, when certain improvements projected are completed, will be thrown into one enclosure, and then Savannah will have a pleasure resort at her very gates, which will be the pride of her citizens and the admiration of strangers. The Park extension has already been improved somewhat by nice walks, and the planting of trees, and addition attraction is now given it as the site of the

CONFEDERATE MONUMENT,

which was completed in April of this year, by the Ladies' Memorial Association of Savannah, and unveiled shortly after, with imposing ceremonies, the entire volunteer military of the city, civic societies and associations participating, an appropriate address being delivered by Hon. Julian Hartridge.

The corner stone of this Monument was laid on the 16 of June, 1874, with Masonic ceremonies, the military being present in force. The ceremonies were opened by prayer from Grand Chaplain Richard Webb, Grand Master Irwin laying the stone. An address was delivered by Hon. Geo. A. Mercer, and the ceremonies were closed by a salute of eleven guns, fired by the Chatham Artillery, the oldest military organization in the State of Georgia.

The Monument cost $25,000, and is built according to a design furnished by Mr. Robert Reid, of Montreal, Canada. In style, the design is modern Italian, and stands about fifty feet in height from the base to the crown of the marble figure, by which it is surmounted. The Monument sets on a terrace of earth work six feet high, by forty feet square, and surrounded by a stone coping; the terrace being reached by stone steps from either of the four facings. On the corners are pedestals which stand out from the Monument proper, and are each graced by a life size marble statue of a soldier on duty.

On the base of the palasters are appropriate mottoes. The front panel on the first stage shows a figure in *alto relievo*, representing the South mourning; the reverse panel shows another figure also in *alto relievo*, of a military character. The two sides or lateral panels, bear inscriptions, one of which is

"To the Confederate Dead;"

the other,

"Come from the four winds, O Breath, and breathe upon these Slain that they may live."—*Ezez.*, xxxii, 9.

Above these panels is a rich cornice supporting trophies representing "Peace and Hope," all carved in bold relief. The next stage shows an open canopy supported on large pilasters, on the centre of which, stands a life size marble statue representing "Silence." Above this is another stage deeply recessed and moulded and ornamented with draped banners, guns, sabres, etc.

The topmost panel is exquisitely paneled and moulded, and forms the base upon which rests the crowning figure—a collosal marble statue representing "Resurrection," or the "Judgment." Garlands, urns, flags, etc., are tastefully carved in appropriate places on the different stages.

The base, coping steps, etc., are of Montreal stone, the main body of the Monument of Pictou (Nova Scotia) sand stone, and the statuary of the very finest Carara marble.

The Monument in point of imposing magnificence, will bear comparison with any in the country.

The main approach to the Park, Bull Street, is the grand promenade boulevard of the city. It is a beautiful wide street, rendered attractive from the Bay to the Park by a series of handsome squares.

In Johnson Square stands the

GREENE MONUMENT,

a noble marble shaft, erected in honor of the Revolutionary hero, General Nathaniel Greene. It was originally intended to place beneath this Monument, the remains of General Greene, and have appropriate inscriptions carved upon the base, but as is pretty well known to every reader of history, the burial place of General Greene has never been discovered. It was ascertained that his body had been placed in a vault in the Old Cemetery, but the place was not marked, from some oversight, and after many years when search was made for it, no trace could be found, and for all time, the grave of the great patriot, will remain unknown. The Monument, however. stands a lasting tribute to his patriotism and devotion.

Chippewa Square, opposite the Theatre, is graced with a very fine fountain, whilst most of the other Squares are ornamented with grassy mounds.

In Monterey Square, stands the beautiful Monument erected in memory of

COUNT PULASKI,

who was killed in the defense of Savannah, near the site now occupied by the Central Railroad Depot buildings. The corner stone of the Monument was laid on the 11th October, 1853, the military under command of Colonel (now General) A. R. Lawton; the various Masonic bodies and the citizens en masse participating. The shaft is fifty feet high, and is surrounded by a statue of "Liberty," holding the banner of the stars and stripes; on the front in relievo, is the statue representing Count Pulaski after he received his mortal wound, in the act of falling from his horse, still grasping his sword. The date of the event, October 9th, 1799, is recorded above.

The corner stone of the Greene Monument, was laid on the 21st March, 1825, by General LaFayette and the Masonic Lodges, and that of the Pulaski Monument, on Chippewa Square, on the same day, but the latter was subsequently removed to Monterey Square, in 1853.

OTHER PLACES OF INTEREST.

It would require considerable space to enumerate in detail other objects of interest to the visitor in Savannah, and hence, only brief mention is made of the most prominent.

The Masonic Temple, corner Whitaker and Liberty Streets, is conceded by visiting brethren, to be the finest and most conveniently arranged of any similar edifice in the country, and beyond doubt, the handsomest in the South.

The stranger will also be interested in visiting Hodgson Memorial Building, corner of Whitaker and Gaston Streets, owned and occupied by the Georgia Historical Society; the Exchange, the various Churches, especially the Independent Presbyterian Church, corner of South Broad and Bull Streets, which was constructed at a cost of over $260,000, and is a magnificent structure.

The Cotton Factory, Paper Factory, Rice Mills, Water Works, the Public Schools, (which are the pride of the State) and the various Benevolent Institutions, that render Savannah noted for charity, afford an opportunity for visitors to pass away their time pleasantly and profitably.

In addition to the various resorts out side the city, along the line of the Savannah, Skidaway and Seaboard Railroad Company, there are other places worth visiting.

Pleasant trips may be made by sail or steamer to

FORT PULASKI,

a few miles down the river, originally built at a cost of $988,859. This Fort, which was the scene of a long seige during the late war, has, under recent appropriations by the Government, been greatly strengthened and improved. The trip to the Fort is pleasant, and can be made within an hour.

DAUFUSKIE ISLAND,

a somewhat historic place, is another point of interest on the coast and is a favorite spot for excursion parties. The Island is some six miles in length, and has ever been noted for the abundance of fish, oysters, crabs, etc., to be obtained in the waters surrounding it. Daufuskie is the Indian name, and it is presumed from the number of mounds, tomahawks and arrow heads that have been discovered, that it was a favorite resort with the festive Red Men. One portion of the Island, the property of Mr. H. M. Stoddard, is known as "Bloody Point," for which name, tradition thus accounts.

The massacre of Bloody Point was previous to the Revolutionary war. The Islands of Port Royal and St. Helena were pretty thickly settled with white population when Hilton Head, Dow Dusky, Pinckney, and the other neighboring Islands were held in possession by a few isolated Indians, or were altogether uninhabited: they formed a kind of neutral ground between the White and Red men. The Indians from Georgia were in the habit of making frequent inroads upon the white settlements, killing the inhabitants, and carrying off whatever plunder they could gather, to their remoter homes in the further south—they formed large war parties, and would proceed as far north as Hilton Head, here they would *skulk* about until a fair chance offered, when they would cross Broad River, and ravage the neighboring settlements—hence the name of Skulk Creek, (and not Skull as is now written.)

The Indians were in the habit of returning to Skulk Creek after these invasions, and would elude pursuit among its numerous nooks and windings. Upon one of these occasions, after having committed a number of murders, and having loaded their canoes with whatever plunder they could collect, and having secured a quantity of "fire water", it is presumed from the sequel, they passed through Skulk Creek on their return south without stopping at their old haunts, and never halted until they reached Dow Dusky, where they thought they would be beyond the reach of the whites.

A very strong and determined party of whites went in pursuit of them. On reaching Hilton Head, they learned from a few Indians, of a friendly tribe, that their enemies had not halted, but had proceeded on south. Having induced these friendly Indians to join them as guides, they continued their pursuit further south; when they had gone as far as Dow Dusky, they discovered from the smoke of their camp, that the Indians had halted at the southeast point of the Island, and had put all their boats a short distance up what now is known as New River, to avoid the surf which breaks at that point; and when the whites landed at the northeastern portion of the Island, the red devils, at the extreme southeast point, were enjoying themselves in an unwonted round of conviviality and feasting. Having effected a safe landing, the

whites moved cautiously and stealthily around the Island, until
they got between the Indians and their boats, thus effectually cut-
ting off the retreat of the savages. The first intimation the Indians had of the presence of the avengers, was a shower of
bullets; they were shot down, bayonetted, sabred and were finally
driven into the sea.

The surprise was complete—the massacre was dreadful—the
white sands were crimson with blood, and the earth was strewn
with wounded, dying and dead, and almost a whole tribe had been
wiped out of existence in a few minutes. A few, very few,
escaped by swimming, some to the opposite marsh, and one swam
to Tybee, a distance of three miles. From the dreadful carnage
at this spot, it received the name of "Bloody Point," which it still
retains at this time, it being the extreme southeastern point of
South Carolina.

After this decisive victory, the settlement to the north of Broad
river received no further molestation from the southern Indians,
and soon after, Hilton Head itself began to be settled by the
whites. The Indians who escaped, having collected after a lapse
of some time, returned to Hilton Head, and finding only two of
the tribe who had guided the whites in their pursuit, avenged
the downfall of their own tribe by destroying both of them;
they then returned south, and were lost sight of ever after—such
is the tradition in St. Luke's.

BEACH HAMMOCK,

or, as it is now known, Arkwright Island, is a favorite point
during the seasons for pic-nics and excursions. There is a fine
wharf at which steamers can land in the roughest sea; a large and
substantial pavilion, and a comfortable hotel a short distance from
the Beach, which is over a mile and a half in length and as firm
and smooth as a parlor floor. Abundance of fish and oysters
can be obtained in the immediate vicinity. The Island is laid off
into lots with a view of making it a summer resort. Some seventy-
six lots have already been taken, and several cottages have already
been erected. Acting upon a proposition of the Proprietor of the
Island, Mr. Thomas Arkwright, the New York Yacht Club have
selected the Hammock as their winter head-quarters, and it is expected during the coming season, will erect at the place suitable
boat houses, etc. In the early spring, tourists will find a trip to
this point pleasant and interesting. A steamer has been purchased

to run exclusively during the season between Savannah and the
Island, occasionally stopping at Thunderbolt and Isle of Hope.

TYBEE ISLAND,

is another sea side resort of rare attraction, and is destined to
become quite a flourishing village in the course of time. It is
some miles further from the city than Beach Hammock, but is
reached by steamers within an hour and a half, the run down
being quite pleasant and interesting.

> "The sea, the sea, the open sea!
> The blue, the fresh and ever free."

The ocean has ever been an object of interest in all its moods,
whether its waves are lashed into fury, or break idly upon the beach
in soothing murmurs. And at Tybee, one can enjoy from the
magnificent beach, the sight of old "Neptune" in his angriest and
most frolicsome moods. Such a beach can scarcely be found on
any sea coast; and many who are familiar with Cape May, Long
Branch, and Atlantic City, pronounce that for a fine beach and
surf, the sea face of Tybee surpasses any of these famous water-
ing places. The beach is six miles long and a third to a quarter
wide, and affords one of the most delightful and charming drives
imaginable. Frequent opportunities are offered for visiting this
point, and tourists should not consider their travels complete
unless they include a trip to one or the other of the places above
named.

THUNDERBOLT,

about five miles from the city, and pleasantly situated upon the
banks of the Thunderbolt river, is the site of two or three hotels,
and a score or so very comfortable private residences. The point
is accessible by a most delightful drive on a shell road, and also
by rail communication.

BONAVENTURE,

or "Evergreen Cemetery," about four miles from the city, is one
of the loveliest spots in the world, possessing peculiar charms
which have no rival in natural beauty and magnificence. This
picturesque place has the same means of communication as Thunderbolt.

GREENWICH PARK,

about four and a half miles from the city. or half a mile southeast from Bonaventure, from which a fine view can be obtained,
is also a very attractive spot, and is the property of the Savannah
Schuetzen Society, and may properly be called the Schuetzen
Park. Its natural beauty has been greatly improved by the Society, and it is the scene of their annual festivals, which of late years
have become "national," so to speak in their character, the
entire populace of the city participating. These festivals generally
occur in April, and thus northern visitors have an opportunity of
visiting the Park when it is the scene of animated life and beauty.

JASPER SPRINGS

is located on the Augusta road, about two miles from the city and
nearly opposite the Fair Grounds of the Agricultural and Mechan-
ical Association of Georgia. It is noted as being the scene of the
bold exploits of Sergeants Jasper and Newton, previous to the
siege of Savannah. Sergeant Jasper, after his gallantry at Fort
Moultrie, was granted a roving commission by Col. Moultrie,
commanding the Second South Carolina Regiment, with the
privilege of reforming his own command. The scouts of Jasper's
were of great assistance to the American army, frequently obtained
valuable information, which could not be procured in any other
way. At one time Jasper came into Savannah, and remained
here several days, during which time he collected valuable information concerning the number and position of the British forces,
and furnished it to General Lincoln. On one occasion Jasper met,
near Ebenezer, a lady named Mrs. Jones, who was in great distress
about her husband. He had taken the oath of allegiance to the
British Government; afterwards joined the American army, and
was captured by the British, who determined to hang him, with
others who were to be carried to Savannah, in fact were then on
their way to the city for that purpose. His sympathies were
aroused, and he promised to rescue him if it were possible. He
consulted Sergeant Newton, who was with him, but no definite
plan was arranged, though they decided to follow the guard, and
take advantage of what opportunity offered for accomplishing
their purposes. Early the next morning, after the interview
between Jasper and Mrs. Jones, a guard of British soldiers, comprising a sergeant, a coporal and eight men, left Ebenezer for Savannah, with the prisoners in irons. The wives and children of

two or three of the prisoners followed. Jasper and Newton kept
on the trail of the party, and upon coming near the Spring, got
ahead of them and hid in the bushes, presuming, and as the sequel
proved correctly, that the guard would halt to get water, and
a chance to rescue the prisoners would be presented. Upon reaching a point in the road opposite the Spring, which was pleasantly
located in a grove, the guard halted and stacked arms, two men
being left with them in charge of the prisoners. The rest of the
guard, not apprehending the slightest danger, went to the Spring.
Jasper and Newton were not slow to appreciate the situation, and
creeping up to the sentinels shot them down, secured the stack of
muskets and called on the guard, (who returned hastily from the
spring upon hearing the fire) to surrender. The Britishers per-
ceiving that they were completely at the mercy of the two determined men, concluded discretion was the better part of valor, and
surrendered. The irons were knocked off the prisoners and
placed upon the soldiers who were conducted to the American
camp at Purysburg. The Spring is at the present time nicely
walled in, and is visited every year by hundreds of strangers on
account of its historical interest. The water is pure and cool.

HISTORICAL NOTES OF SAVANNAH.

As every visitor to a city desires to learn something of its past,
as well as of its present and possible future, it is quite *appropos*
that a few historical notes should appear in connection with this
sketch of the suburban resorts of Savannah. With these notes,
which are presented succinctly and briefly, will also be found
an interesting account of the nomenclature of the different wards
of the city. This information will enable the visitor to write or
speak more understandingly of the city and community in which
he has sojourned, and being presented in this form, he obtains
multum in parvo.

SETTLEMENT OF SAVANNAH.

The first settlement of Savannah was made in the month of
February, 1733, by General Oglethorpe and some thirty families.
On the 7th of July following, the settlers assembled on the
strand, (the Bay) for the purpose of designating the lots. In a
devotional service, they united in thanksgiving to God, "that the
lines had fallen to them in a pleasant place, and that they were
about to have a good heritage." The wards and tithings were

then named, each ward consisting of four tithings, and each tithing of ten houses, and a house and lot was given to each free-holder.

After a dinner, provided by the Governor, the grant of a Court of Record was read, and the officers were appointed. The session of the magistrates was then held, a jury impaneled, and a case tried. This jury was the first impaneled in Georgia.

The town was governed by three baliffs, and had a recorder, register, and a town court holden every six weeks, where all matters, civil and criminal, were decided by grand and petit juries, as in England. No lawyers were allowed to plead for hire, nor attorneys to take money, but (as in old times in England) every man could plead his own cause.

The Rev. Messrs. John and Charles Wesley came over in 1736. On Sunday, the 7th March of that year, John Wesley preached for the first time in America. His text was from the Epistle for the day—13 chapter, 1st Corinthians—and Christain Charity his theme.

In May 1738, the Rev. Geo. Whitfield, the celebrated preacher, arrived, accompanied by James Habersham. Mr. H. was afterwards President of the Orphan House, and President of His Majesty's Council in Georgia, and in 1744, together with Charles Harris, established the first commercial house in Georgia. In 1749, they loaded the first ship for England—exports, pitch, tar, rice and deer skins—value, $10.000.

NOTED INCIDENTS.

In October, 1741, the government of the colony was changed from bailiffs to trustees.

In 1750, the number of white persons in Georgia was computed at about 1,500.

A public Filature was erected in 1751, on a lot in Reynolds ward, where now stands a block of buildings known as Cassell Row. It remained for some forty years as a filature or manufactory of silk; afterwards it was used as a City Hall and a public house, and was destroyed by fire in 1839.

The first Royal Governor of Georgia, John Reynolds, Esq., arrived in Savannah in October, 1754.

Sir James Wright, the last of the Royal Governors, was appointed about the year 1761, and held the office until he was forced to flee in 1775.

The first printing press was established in 1763, and the "Georgia Gazette," printed on the 7th April of that year.

Robert Bolton, Esq., the first Post Master of Savannah, was appointed in 1764, by Benjamin Barron, Esq., Post Master General of the Southern District of America.

In 1766 the city consisted of 400 dwelling houses, a church, an independent meeting house, a council house, a court house, and a filature.

It had also, two suburbs—Yamacraw and Trustees' Gardens, (a place where the Trustees had a famous garden laid out, in order to make experiments before they were advised to be accounted objects profitable to be introduced.)

The same year the city had three fine libraries, in which were works in almost all languages.

In 1770, the city extended on the west, to what is now Jefferson street; on the east, to what is now Lincoln street, and on the south, to what is now South Broad street; and contained six squares, and twelve streets, besides the Bay.

On the 5th June, 1775, the first liberty pole was erected in Savannah, at Peter Tondee's, who kept a public house on the spot now occupied by Jones' range.

The first attack by the British on Savannah, was made on the 3d March, 1776. It ended in the discomfiture of the regulars under Majors Maitland and Grant.

On the 29th December, 1788, Savannah was taken by the British.

In October, 1779, an unsuccessful attempt was made by the French and American armies to recapture Savannah from the British. Count D'Estaing and General Lincoln were the commanders. 637 of French and 241 of the continentals and militia were killed and wounded. In this attack Pulaski fell; the spot where he was shot down is about one hundred rods from the present Depot of the Central Railroad.

The headquarters of the English, while in Savannah, were at the house on Broughton street, now occupied by S. C Dunning, Esq.

Governor Wright's house was on the lot in Heathcote ward, where now the "Telfair house" stands.

On the 11th July, 1783, Savannah was formally given up by the British to the Americans, and Col. James Jackson, the father of the Col. Joseph W. Jackson, was selected by General Wayne to receive the surrender of the same from the British commander. The American army entered it the same day.

The first session of the Legislature of the State was held in Savannah in January, 1784, in the brick house now standing in South Broad street, between Drayton and Abercorn streets. This building was afterwards occupied as a public house, and long known as "Eppinger's Ball Room." It is the oldest brick house in Savannah. Dr. Lyman Hall was then Governor.

In 1786, died, near Savannah, General Nathaniel Greene, a Major General of the Revolution, and "the beloved General" of Washington. Immediately after the peace of 1783, General Greene settled in Georgia, the State having liberally granted to him valuable property in the vicinity of Savannah. The General visited the city on the 12th of June, and returned home on the 14th : the same day he was attacked with *coup de soleil*, and died on the 19th. His body was brought to Savannah on the 20th, and buried in a vault the same day. In a search made in the year 1820 for his remains, owing to some strange oversight at the time of his interment in not designating them, or from lapse of years, they could not be found, and "no man knoweth his sepulchure to this day."

In December, 1789, a law was passed by the legislature making Savannah a city.

The first Mayor (elected in 1790) was John Houstoun. Wm. B. Bulloch, was elected Mayor in 1809. Col. James Hunter, was elected Alderman in 1806.

In May, 1791, General Washington visited, in the course of his Southern tour, the city of Savannah. He was received with a military display, addressed by a variety of bodies, and other demonstrations, public and private, were made to evince the popular joy and satisfaction at his visit. The house in which lodgings were prepared for him, on the northwest corner of Barnard and State streets, is still standing.

In November, 1796, the first destructive fire occurred in Savannah. It broke out in a bake house in market square, and destroyed 229 houses, besides out houses, etc. Estimated loss of property, one million of dollars.

In May, 1814, arrived in the waters of Savannah, the U. S. sloop of war Peacock, Lewis Warrington commander, bringing in as a prize H. B. M. brig of War Epervier, Captain Wales, of 18 guns. The E. had on board $110,000 in specie which was condemned and distributed according to law. She was built in 1812, and was one of the finest vessels of her class in the British navy.

In April, 1819, arrived the steamship Savannah, from New York. This steamer was projected and owned in Savannah, and was the first steamship built in the United States, and the first that ever crossed the Atlantic. She left Savannah in May for Liverpool, and afterwards proceeded to St. Petersburg.

In May of this year, James Monroe, the fifth President of the United States, visited Savannah, accompanied by Mr. Calhoun, Secretary of War, General Gaines and others. He was received with a southern welcome.

In December of this year, 1819, departed this life, in the 14th year of his ministry, and in the midst of his usefulness, Henry Kollock, D. D., the esteemed and eloquent Pastor of the Independent Presbyterian Church of Savannah. Dr. K. was indeed, "a burning and shining light," and faithfully fulfilled the arduous duties of pastor and teacher to his large congregation.

In January, 1820, occurred the largest fire which ever ravaged the city. It commenced on the east side of Old Franklin ward. 463 buildings were destroyed, besides out buildings. Loss upwards of $4,000,000.

In March, 1825, General LaFayette visited Savannah. He was received with every demonstration of regard as the nation's friend in the time of need, and as the nation's guest.

PARTICULARS RESPECTING THE WARDS.

Anson Ward, is one of the old wards of the city—named after Lord Anson, the celebrated navigator; its square, containing one acre, is named Oglethorpe Square.

Brown Ward, was laid out in 1815, and named after Jacob Brown, a General in the U. S army. Its square, containing one and a half acres, is named Chippewa Square, after the Plains of Chippewa, a place memorable to the Americans arms in the war of 1812, and where General Brown was a distinguished actor.

Columbia Ward, was laid out soon after the Revolution. Its square, bearing the same name, contains in its enclosure three-fourths of an acre.

Crawford Ward, was laid out in 1843, and named after William H. Crawford, a distinguished son of Georgia. Its square bears the same name, and contains in its enclosure three-quarters of an acre.

Derby Ward, one of the old wards of the city, is named after James, Earl of Derby, one of the contributors to the Trustees' Funds. Its square, called Johnson Square, after a friend of the

Colony, Governor Johnson, of South Carolina, contains one and a half acres, and has in its enclosure the Greene Monument, of which mention is made in another place. In this ward are situated Christ Church, the Central Railroad and Banking Company, the City Exchange, containing the City Offices, Post Office and Custom House, the Pulaski House and the City Hotel.

Decker Ward, one of the old wards of the city, is named after Sir Matthew Decker, one of the commissioners to collect funds for the Trustees, and who himself contributed £150. Its square, named Elllis Square after Governor Ellis, contains one acre, and since the year 1823 has been used as the City Market, over which spacious and comfortable buildings have been erected.

Elbert Ward, laid out soon after the Revolution, is named after General Samuel Elbert, Governor of the State of Georgia in 1785. Its square, bearing the same name, contains three-fourths of an acre.

Franklin Ward, (old) is named after Benjamin Franklin. Its square, bearing the same name, contains three-fourths of an acre.

Franklin Ward, (new) is an irregular plat, comprising all that part of the city north of the Bay, by lines from Old Franklin, has no public square or public buildings.

Greene Ward, is named after Maj. General Nathaniel Greene, of the Revolutionary war. Its square, bearing the same name, contains three-fourths of an acre.

Heathcote Ward, one of the old wards of the city, is named after the family of Heathcotes, friends and benefactors of the Colony. Its square, containing one acre, is called St. James' Square.

Jackson Ward, is named after General Jackson. Its square, containing one acre, is called Orleans Square, and has in it a public cistern for the use of the Fire Department.

Jasper Ward, is named after Sergeant Jasper of the war of the Revolution. Its square, containing one acre, is called Madison Square, after the late President Madison.

LaFayette Ward, named after General LaFayette. Its square, containing one acre, bears the same name.

Liberty Ward, laid out soon after the Revolution. Its square, containing three-fourths of an acre, bears the same name.

Monterey Ward, laid out in 1847, and named after the city of Monterey in Mexico. Its square, containing one acre, bears the same name, and is the site of the Puliski Monument.

Oglethorpe Ward, is one of the old wards of the city, named

after General Oglethorpe; it consists of all that part of the city west of West Broad street from the Railroad Depot to the river. It has no public square. In this ward are situated the Depot of the Central Railroad Company, covering, with its offices, work-store-houses, etc., ten acres, the depot or terminus of the Savannah and Ogeechee Canal.

Percival Ward, one of the old wards of the city, named after Lord Viscount Percival, President of the Trustees. Its square, contains one acre, and is called Wright Square, after Governor Wright. In this ward are situated the Court House, the Evangelical Lutheran Church, the Second Babtist Church, the Chatham Artillery's Armory Hall.

Pulaski Ward, is named after Count Pulaski. Its square contains one acre, and bears the same name.

Reynolds Ward, one of the old wards of the city, named after Governor Reynolds. Its square contains one acre, and bears the same name.

Warren Ward, is named after General Joseph Warren, of the war of the Revolution. Its square contains three-fourths of an acre, and bears the same name.

Washington Ward, was laid out soon after the Revolution. Its square contains three-fourths of an acre, and bears the same name.

On November 6th, 1872, an ordinance was passed laying off into wards certain portions of the southern suburbs, and designating them as follows :

Lee Ward, named in honor of General Robert E. Lee, the great soldier and patriot of the second Revolution.

Padelford Ward, named for the late Edward Padelford, a wealthy and distinguished merchant of Savannah.

Johnston Ward, is named after General Joseph E. Johnston, the distinguished southern soldier, now an honored resident of Savannah.

Kelly Ward, named for Eugene Kelly.   .

Teltair Ward, named after Governor Edward Telfair.

Mercer Ward, after General H. W. Mercer.

Schley Ward, after the late Dr. Jno. Schley, an eminent physician of Savannah.

Haywood Ward, after Hon. Alfred Haywood, then Chairman of Council.

Weed Ward, after the late Henry D. Weed, a merchant of Savannah for over fifty years.

Waring Ward, after the owner of the property, Dr. J. J. Waring.

Atlantic Ward and Canal ward.

Curry Town District, is all that portion of the city extending south from Liberty street between Tatnall street and the western limits It has no public squares.

DEFENCES OF SAVANNAH.

During the war, there were four lines of defence adopted, of these, three were constructed, and the fourth abandoned, after an inconsiderable amount of work had been done.

The first or exterior Line of Defence, was constructed early in the war, to protect our coast from attacks by the Federal Navy, and to prevent the landing of troops. This line extended from Caustons Bluff, four miles east of Savannah, to the Ogeechee River, and embraced the following points, at which works were erected : Greenwich, Thunderbolt, Isle of Hope, Beaulieu, and Rosedew. Detached works were also constructed on Whitmarsh, Oatland, Skidaway, and Green Islands, but these latter works were only occupied a portion of the time, and towards the close of the war, were mostly abandoned. The general character of works at the points mentioned, were water batteries, constructed of earth, and reveted with sand bags, sods, and facines, with traverses, bomb proofs, etc. The armament of these works, generally consisted of heavy ordnance en-barbette. Where rifle guns and columbiads could not be procured, smooth bore 42 and 60 pounders were used, and occasionally 8 and 10 inch morters were employed. The river batteries, located at, and around Fort Jackson, were intended for the protection of our main water approach, and to constitute, as it were, the extreme left of the before mentioned line. Prominent among the works referred to was Fort Bartow at Caustons Bluff. This was the largest and most complete work on our entire coast, and the character of the work and labor expended in its construction, attested the importance attached to this position, as a salient point on this line, and so to speak, the key to Savannah. This was a bastioned work, enclosing area of seventeen acres, with glacis, moat, curtains, and in fact every appointment complete, bomb proofs and surgeon rooms under ground, with advanced batteries and rifle pits in front near water line. The other works on this line, were not from their character, derserving of special notice. Fort Bartow was pronounced by some of our ablest officers, a splended work, and recognized by all as the most important in the defences of Savannah. This work was constructed by Capt. M. B. Grant, of the Engineer Corps, who also had immediate charge of a considerable portion of the work around the city.

Fort McAlister, located on the south side of the Ogeechee River at Genisis Point, was an enclosed work, of about one acre, detached and isolated, irregular in form, but compactly built, and adapted to its isolated condition and surroundings. The armament of this work was heavy, and the gallant and successful defence repeatedly made here against the enemy's iron clads, and at the last to one of Sherman's corps from the land side, have given it a name and place in the History of Savannah's defences, that is imperishable and preeminently grand. Though a little and insignificant earth work, it was by location and circumstances called upon to act a giant's part. On this exterior line, there were no other points deserving special notice.

The second line constructed, was what was known as the interior line of defence. This line was almost semicircular in contour, and distant from the city, on an average of three-fourths of a mile; its left resting at Fort Boggs, next to the rice lands on the Savannah River; its right resting at a point a little south of Laurel Grove Cemetery, and on the low lands of the Springfield Plantation. This line as the term interior signifiies, was to resist any direct assault upon the city, should a force succeed in passing the exterior line. This line consisted of detached lunettes at regular intervals, constructed with mutual flank defence, and having sectors of fire, covering the entire space in front of the line, all growth having been cut away for a half mile in advance. The curtains were not of the same heavy character as the lunettes, but consisted of rifle pits and covered ways for direct communication. Abatis were constructed in front of many of the lunettes. No portion of this line was ever subjected to an attack, and there was nothing to create or give distinction to any special lunettes. There were, however, on this line certain works which should be mentioned, viz:

Fort Boggs, on the left of the line, was a bastioned work, enclosed (commonly known as a star fort,) about an acre and a half in area. It was situated on the Bluff, in a commanding position, and would have proved a very strong and important work had it been attacked.

Fort Brown, near the Catholic Cemetery, was a point of some

importance on this line, more however, from its early location and construction than any special merit.

This interior line would have proved formidable, had circumstances required a test. Most of these lunettes have been removed or leveled since the war.

It was not until the early part of 1864, that it was thought necessary to fortify Savannah inland (west) when the Federals were meeting with successes in the west, and gradually approaching the coast. It was at this juncture that a line of defence was adopted and constructed on the west of Savannah; the right of this line resting at Williamson's place, on the Savannah River, four miles from the city; the left resting on Salt Creek, near Barkley's place, about seven miles from the city. This line consisted of detached works, continuously connected with rifle pits. The natural defence on this line was very great; the swamps and low lands on the front of the line in many places being impracticable, and making it difficult of approach. This was the line upon which the defence of Savannah was made for eight days, and maintained successfully against Sherman's hordes. The fighting over this line was simultaneous and uninterrupted over the whole front, and the most conspicuous point, upon which the Federals seemed to con', centrate, and which they repeatedly assaulted, was Daily's farm, near the Ogeechee Canal. Repeated, but unsuccessful assaults were also made upon the right of the line at Williamson's. Savannah was successfully evacuated, while a mere picket's guard held this line unknown to the enemy.

Upon the near approach of Sherman, it was deemed advisable to construct a still more advanced line, west of the city; whereupon a line was adopted, extending from Montieth, on the Savannah River, to the Ogeechee River, a distance of about 14 miles. This line had no natural defence whatever, the whole country in front being practicable, and was so reported by the Engineer in charge, Capt. Grant. If constructed, it must be artificial, without natural aid, and it was found impracticable to construct the line in the short time between its inception, and the arrival of Sherman, it was therefore abandoned, and the fight made at the inner or original line. It was Capt. Grant's opinion that under no circumstances could this line have been held (if it had been completed) against such fearful odds.

The great natural advantages of the inner line alone, which enabled our comparatively small force to hold it, even for eight days.

The ruins of many of these fortifications may yet be seen at different points around the city.

AN EVENT OF THE SEASON.

Prominent among the many delightful and successful amusement schemes at Isle of Hope, during the season, was a great Spelling Bee on the 24th of July, 1875, which proved a mammoth affair, fraught with mirth, merriment and humor. As an evidence of the estimation in which the affair was held, the following very interesting and graphic account is taken from the

[Savannah Morning News, July 36.]

THE GREAT SPELLING BEE—IMMENSE SUCCESS AND A GLORIOUS TIME—ISLE OF HOPE ALIVE WITH FUN AND MERRIMENT.

General Ticket Agent Bren and Superintendent Haines, of the Savannah, Skidaway and Seaboard Railroad Company, have every reason to feel gratified at the overwhelming success which attended their inauguration of a Spelling Bee and Tournament at Isle of Hope yesterday afternoon. It was without doubt the biggest success of the season, and few projects for the amusement of our people have been attended with more satisfactory results or earned more popular favor.

Throughout the day the various trains carried out large numbers of people, but, as was anticipated, the 3:25 train made the trip of the day. Thirteen coaches were taxed to their utmost capacity to accommodate the visitors, and probably several hundred more would have gone, had it been posible to carry them, as groups were left disconsolate on various street corners. It had been expected that the crowd would be great, as more than ordinary interest had been felt in the "Bee," but we doubt if the enterprising originators had any conception of the multitude which flocked to this favorite resort.

The elegant platform was crowded, and at one time it was almost impossible to move through the throngs gathered to discuss the approaching contest and its probable results. It is estimated that with the addition of those brought down by the 3:25 train, there were fully two thousand five hundred people on the ground, the largest crowd that has ever been seen at Isle of Hope on any occasion, the Fourth of July regatta not excepted.

After the arrival of this train preparations were made for the contest. Owing to the crowd, it was with some difficulty that space was cleared for the formation of the class of misses. But Superintendent Haines was equal to the emergency, and with the assistance of Mr. W. S. Bogart, Mr. J. S. F. Lancaster, Capt. John Cooper and others, a rope was stretched and a kind of "pen" constructed. The crowd, however, were very eager to get close enough to hear the spelling, and, per consequence, a considerable amount of genteel scrouging was done. In due time, however, all arrangements were perfected. The contestants, numbering thirty-five bright and sanguine young misses, were ranged in a circle, and Mr. Bogart, in a few explanatory remarks upon the subject of spelling,

OPENED THE CONTEST.

At the first word the head of the class disappeared, and in a few seconds had many companions. It would require too much space to present a list of the words given, suffice it that it comprised alone words in general use, Mr. Bogart avoiding giving strictly technical words, or those relating exclusively to the arts' and sciences. The excitement was very great, and increased as the contestants dwindled in numbers. At last the result was announced amidst applause, and the following young misses declared winners of the prizes annexed respectively:

Miss Emma Sollee, first prize, as the best speller—Silver Cup, presented by the Savannah, Skidaway and Seaboard Railroad Company.

Miss Hennie Haym, second prize, as the second best speller—Elegant selection of Music, presented by Ludden & Bates.

Miss Dora Procter, third prize, as the third best speller—Elegant Croquet set, presented by J. M. Cooper & Co.

Miss Mary Maddox, fourth prize, as the fourth best speller—Half-dozen Wenck's Extract, presented by O. Butler & Co.

THE YOUNG LADIES' CONTEST.

The contest for the misses having been concluded, the contestants for the first class prizes were called to the floor, and about forty young ladies responded. The greatest interest was felt in this "Bee," owing to the fact that the prizes were more valuable, as also that the contestants were young ladies. This contest was likewise conducted by Mr. Bogart, and was quite a lively affair, the issue being anticipated with rare eagerness. The possession of so valuable and useful a prize as a fine Singer Sewing Machine was no small matter, and there was a general anxiety to learn who would be the fair and fortunate victor. This "Bee" lasted about twenty-five minutes, and resulted as follows:

CLASS NO. 1.

Miss Jennie Lowenthall, first prize, as the best speller—Elegant Singer Sewing Machine, presented by C. A. Vosburgh, Manager.

Miss Sheftall, second prize, as the second best speller—Elegant Work-Box, presented by S. P. Hamilton.

Miss Heidt, third prize, as the third best speller—Half-dozen Ladies' Silk Scarfs, presented by H. C. Houston.

Miss Miriam L. Solomon, fourth prize, as the fourth best speller—Toilet Set, presented by J. S. Silva.

THE BOYS' BEE.

In order to get through with the "Bee," that the visitors might have an opportunity to otherwise enjoy themselves, it was decided to inaugurate the contest for boys whilst that of the young ladies was in progress. Accordingly, those boys who desired to enter the class, were assembled under the large tree on the bluff, south of the dancing pavilion, and Mr. J. F. S. Lancaster took the conduct of the contest. Twenty-nine boys entered, many of whom stood their ground well and showed considerable proficiency in orthography. After a spirited contest, the prize, a handsome Silver Watch, valued at $25, offered by the Railroad Company, was awarded to Master Hugo Platen. Master J. Mac being pronounced the second best speller.

The " Bee" over, preparations were commenced for the inauguration of the

BLINDMANS' BUFF TOURNAMENT,

which proved provocative of much mirth to the old as well as the young. The course was laid off in the road in front of Mr. Buckingham's residence, the distance being about thirty yards; at the head was suspended a large ring, and the young knights, numbering thirty-six, were in turn brought to the front, and had their eyes bandaged with a towel, and being armed with a wand, were told to go for the ring, and they went, in many instances with the most ludicrous results. The tournament was managed in the most satisfactory manner by Dr. W. R. Waring and Superintendent Haines, and lasted probably three-quaters of an hour, when all the knights were ruled off except four—Masters John Dillon, M. C. Proctor, Robert Spivy and J. Mac, each of whom had carried the ring successfully. The contest therefore lay between these four for the possession of the prize. Masters Mac and Proctor being dropped out on the first "run," Masters Spivy and Dillon contested for the prize, and after two ties between them, Master Dillon came out the victor, and was declared entitled to the prize, a very elegant Silver Cup, offered by the Railroad. There was some dissatisfaction among the little fellows at the result, and owing to this and the absence of Superintendent Haines, who had been compelled to leave the ground on business, the prize was not presented, and the decision will be considered, though it is likely Master Dillon will receive the prize.

CLOSE OF THE DAY.

The shades of night were falling as the sports were brought to a close, and the 6:20 p. m. train for the city having arrived, those who were desirous of reaching home early, left the pleasant scenes. The temptation to remain later, however, induced the great majority to wait for the next train, which was announced to leave Isle of Hope at 7:35 p. m. The interim was spent in dancing, promenading, etc., and a more enjoyable time could not have been desired. The universal expression was one of satisfaction, and the experience of all seemed to be of the most pleasant character. The amusements were pronounced *par excellence*, and the arrangements for comfort and entertainment of the visitors could not have been better. Mr. Buckingham, with an able corps of assistants, had his hands full, but was able to supply all with everything needful in the liquid refreshment line. The dining-room was well patronized, and the efficient colored cook, Maggie, managed to serve up, in a remarkable short time, numerous excellent suppers of fresh fish, soft shell crabs, etc. Altogether, there was nothing in any of the arrangements that failed to give satisfaction, and mine host, Buckingham, was voted a trump.

The transportation of such an immense crowd was no easy job, and the admirable manner in which it was done reflected great credit upon the management of the indefatigable and courteous Superintendent.

Taken all in all, the affair yesterday may be recorded in the history of Isle of Hope as one of the most charming and delightful that has ever marked any gathering for amusement at that place.

www.ingramcontent.com/pod-product-compliance
Lightning Source LLC
Chambersburg PA
CBHW021456090426
42739CB00009B/1755